WE ARE ALWAYS & FOREVER ENDING

Earle

ISBN: 978-1-913642-87-7

Book designed by Aaron Kent

Edited by Aaron Kent

Broken Sleep Books (2021), Talgarreg, Wales

Contents

The End of *You*

The End of *Us*

The End of the *World*

The End of *Everything*

We Are Always & Forever Ending

Adrian B. Earle

To Vinita,
I am all of my love & I am yours

The End of *You*

Wave Upon Wave

Light trips proud.
Standing water
striped with sand
strewn with ripples
eiderdowns for striders
gilded by the deep.

Eyeless tight
                    a push
a lunar pallor
brightens
swirl and gyre
bringing gentle
waves that leave me
as they always do
deeper in the
shifting mire.

Still, it's sudden,
the chill that skips
to kiss my thighs
as more unfaithful
water rushes
in.

Forgive us our trespasses

They worked here once / you can tell because / The darkness
undulates / the repetition of industry / the remaining half of
sign says NIBS / I like to think this is where favourite pens
were born / now here I'm reluctant to leave /cable trailing /
yards & yards of brilliant shards / descending mote like on
the battered air / thick with cold & huddled close to
camphor / a pitted pungent marrow bone / of rotted work
top trains away / to abrupt and ragged caesurae / tools
suspended mid-strike / hammers held high fifty years since
the power went out / since the jobs found wings / value
hungry / casing sheds / itself & purpose / anything too big
to shift sloughs rust / a deep organic peeling / eminent decay
of bleached brick black on grey / a dark stain with wings &
I / share a room that fed fifty families / a room frowning in
reproach / at my casual break & enter / the lintel of the eye I
climbed in through / raised in question / you with your tools
& efforts & sweat? / you with your hope? / Who are you?
who the fuck are you? / there is nothing for you here / there
was nothing / pens without ink then / now not even that /

Inheritance

My Grandad gave my young father a grenade.
& once he'd gripped it tightly in his fist
my grandad pulled the pin, said 'Be a man'

My father, perhaps in fear, shame, or belief
it was the bomb that made him something.
Lived his life with death gripped in his hand.

When old enough, I moved away, became estranged.
He sent a gift. For decades of hard words, cold glares, callousness
& thrift. He sent a biscuit tin, so poorly wrapped,

within a leaden thing. I open up to find an old MK II
its clip held by the lid. I had no choice, I grasped
to stop the fuse. I couldn't see a pin. Instead,
I found a folded note:

Don't ever say I gave you nothing.

"There's this idea that hierarchical structures are a sociological construct of the Western patriarchy. And that is so untrue that it's almost unbelievable. I use the lobster as an example: We diverged from lobsters evolutionary history about 350 million years ago. Common ancestor. And lobsters exist in hierarchies. They have a nervous system attuned to the hierarchy. And that nervous system runs on serotonin, just like our nervous system do. The nervous system of the lobster and the human being is so similar that anti-depressants work on lobsters. And it's part of my attempt to demonstrate that the idea of hierarchy has absolutely nothing to do with socio-cultural construction, which it doesn't."

> - Jordan Peterson's interview with Cathy Newman for Channel 4, 2018

Autodidact

-To the 'intellectual manosphere'

I

A man smarter than me once said "To be in love is to create
a religion whose God is fallible." The man

was Valéray. I think

    he had a point.

A woman smarter than me once said "A woman needs a man
like a fish needs a bicycle". The woman

was Irina Dunn. I think

    she had a point.

A smarter man than me once said "A Man without God
is like a Fish without a Bicycle". The Man

was Charles S Harris & I think

    he had a point?

So, now

I am trying to decide if this means in my Love, I worship
a fallible fish?

Or that in our Love, one of us is the bicycle?

Or, whether Love by its very existence proves the existence of a God?

Or, whether a bicycle can love a fish God enough to become
indispensable?

I wrote a post about a book I hadn't the time to
finish. I have the time of course, I'm organised.
Just not the time

to spend with books that have no *meaning,*
nor time to spend with people that have no
meaning. The comments

informed me, graciously, I'd wasted time that all
books are figments of imagination, mere concepts.
That time was a flat circle.

That we were somnambulant, all of us except
those men who had chosen our own path, over the
prescriptions of [m]others.

Medication' a further figment fabricated to
alleviate my lack of direction. They want us
medicated not *pilled*,

They want us vaccinated. No. to be clean I need
only know my philosophy, watch the greats
livestream, know thyself – someone said, "for they
have forgotten God"- said someone else.
& they

were *right.* I liked & subscribed because they were
so right. When they said to tidy my room, find
order in the chaos. Respect the hierarchy, they
were right. That 'Rejection of the outer, the other

Is the core principle of man's philosophy' & this
man in his

Alpha pinstripe suit & His authority & His eBook
was beyond the ken of mere mortals, too
indoctrinated to know that they were false,

& I was amongst the righteous, & my truth was the only truth, & I would be loved & Powerful & all the false truths would cease to be recognised once

the great men make their stand & with the guidance of the Man they'd cleanse the world & they were liars, all the females & their ways & minds & all the authors of the books that made no sense.

But the Man said not to worry. They had simply forgotten God & the ways of the Lobster.

I think he has a point.

Oblivion Hymn #1

Oh—hold me as the fire dies, I need
to breathe covalent closeness of two lives
vibrant, lived shimmering, bereft
of longing as only those truly hopeless
could fathom living, we should
shift as we embrace, transform become
fox-formed, vulpine, sleek to rule
the coming dusk, the ever night & we
will be the bright-eyed shiver in the
guttering torchlight, brushed bronze
a child's scream, a pattering, then gone.

BREACH

It is with considerable difficulty that I remember the original era
of my being; all the events of that period appear confused and
indistinct. A strange multiplicity of sensations seized me, and I
saw, felt, heard, and smelt at the same time; and it was,
indeed, a long time before I learned to distinguish between
the operations of my various senses. By degrees, I remember, a
stronger light pressed upon my nerves, so that I was obliged to
shut my eyes. Darkness then came over me and troubled me,
but hardly had I felt this when, by opening my eyes, as I now
suppose, the light poured in upon me again.
– Frankenstein, Mary Shelley, Ch 11.

Not one of us – black or white – knows how to walk when we get
here. Not one of us knows how to open a window, unlock a door.
Not one of us can master a staircase. We are absolutely ignorant
of the almost certain results of falling out of a five-story window.
None of us comes here knowing enough not to play with fire.
Nor can one of us drive a tank, fly a jet, hurl a bomb, or plant a
tree.
– Dark Days, James Baldwin

[Mother]

Those of us who could, we felt remorse.
                        Some of us begged, others still, a stalwart.
Few cried innocence until the last,
                        the final inch of rope gave some relief.
Some of us are truly unrepentant.
                        We will kill again, we vowed we would.
Some of us hunger still to have the chance.
                        Given this sudden wakening in the void.
Some of us lift arms we do not have.
                        While one of us despairs unnatural loud,
as loudly as tumescent flesh can howl.
                        One of us, a heart that keens and sobs
cries through a foreign throat of many throats.
                        Stitched to layer vocal folds as petals,
each exhale sounds as gale winds through a roof.
                        Some of us mistake this polyphony,
as further company, in this crude womb.
                        We always thought of hell as dark and cold,
thought sinners from the furthest light of god
                        but those of us of sin are warmed & light.
Salvation? this strange immobile parody of life?
                        Some of us claim we crave the dark.
We yearn to quietly fall back to that dark.
                        We rage that we were promised death, not *this*
this mocking of wholeness, this agony
                        this.

[Thought]

This is a flicker; this is the turning heads of wildflowers to the sun. Piecemeal at first and then immutable, a revolutionary wave. *This* is soul composed of phantom pain. Pectoral, effluvious ache. A dozen or more sufferings dragged back to the surface like old love. This is a chorus melding in the amniotic. A placental heartbeat. Keeping time with *theirs*. With *hers*. No, *his*. No. With mine. *This* is such burning in limbs comprised of strapped on muscle, knitted vein & memories of what we used to be before the... *This* is the most perfect understanding of the nature of machine flesh has ever realised. Greater than the sum of its parts. *This* is eleven or so nothings becoming one. The one is screaming.

[lightning]

voltaic thrashing
bound in skin
then shutting
embola push forth

choking us
a wretched retching
figure forms
i howl & gag &

flushing alchemy
through cords a thick
black ichor in my throat
convulsions fit

i scream & claw
a howl & writhe
& hurl and spit
to shake & howl

the sky a roar
a roar to rip
the meat apart
a wail in echo

& hurl & sob
i sob & gag
& moan & sleep
drownéd dreck

beyond the hurt
a shower fall
of brightest stars
my second skin

i crawl and weep
when suddenly
i see the stars
is skin, is Skin

[Moon]

Bright pit
        in dark
                so open.
                      Bright,
                            big hole,
                                  warm & bright.
                                        Far as hope

in cold slick
        dark, so high.
                No sound
                      but thump
                            & suck
                                  & thump.
                                      Far bright pit,

no sound
        just open.
                Dark hope,
                      cold dark
                            hope just
                                  Dark. No
                                      sound
                                            & this

bright hole,
        so open
                thump & suck
                      & thump & pull
                          & pull & i,
                                i need
                                    to reach
                                        that safe

bright hole.
      i need
          to crawl
               back in.
                    i do not
                        want dark
                            & thump

& suck
      & wet.
          & i am wet
               & high
                    bright pit
                        is dry
                              i

am small
      & high
          bright pit
               is big
                    Dark is fear
                      & whispers
                            sound
                                  like *night*

Pit is bright,
      whispers
          speak of
               moon

Moon is bright
      & high
          & safe
               & far.
                    Night
                        is dark
                            & fear
                                  & so, i run.

Judges 14:14

"He replied,
'Out of the eater, something to eat;
out of the strong, something sweet.'
For three days they could not give the answer."
-Judges 14:14

Tendrils of honeysuckle probe up
    inside my thigh to where the meat
of manhood lay, though she
    like me is a visitor to this ash
her seeds drifted as I did
    through the summer, & years before
I took root.
    The country, turning as we all do
to dusk, uplifts an ochre musk
    My caresser, she sings her scent
in harmony with hydrangea reaching
    Magdalene towards suspended soles
weeping violet quietly at my feet
    their chorus melds so sweetly
with the rot, where I not
    so far from sense it would be
beautiful.
    They did not intend beauty of me,
Yet, nature disregards concerns of man
    saplings tear their capitols asunder,
ascend the lowly negro to a God.
    Leaf fall will prove me evergreen.
I have seen it, until then
    Carolean bustle in and out of ribs,
make a queen cell of desiccated ventricle.
    Building a palace
in the common wanderer whom in turn
    found a throne in the forest air.
of a cooling dawn. The corvid made
    Prometheus of me
grey down crowns of youth
    slick with courage

their chuckles disturbing
        my subjects iridescent, clustering
about the silent edict
        of my mouth, I am alive.
To the calliphorid, I am life.
        Father to multitudes, ancestor
to millions more.
        On earth, alone and hated.
Now, elevated, I am a nation.
        Midsummer brought the first war
in the country of me.
        Drones driving back the blowfly.
Culling their wriggling young.
        Then peace in the warmly fading days
suckle bound and blooming.
        I drip unctuous with the labour of my colony
Longinus spear wound weeping sugar.
        Unlike the lamb, I fought
No voice in the garden
        Quieted me to fate, instead
I was brough high as they would a Lion
        each of them bleeding, spitting with regret.
They laid out, spent with effort
        beneath my ash crowned glory
The closest to divinity they could get.
        Now I am hollow, verdant,
regal, dripping as is fitting.
        The source of sweetness, strength.

NO SOUP

The darkness beyond the threshold is complete. It breathes. A slab of nothingness where a cupboard used to be. Not a can or carton to be found. She reaches left into the murk for the light switch she knows is on the wall at shoulder height, only to feel her fingers curl around the pillar of the frame into that nothingness. She notices it is cool and slightly damp. She notices in that same long second that the floor has absented itself.

The usual olive cracked linoleum, the single sheet that had somehow gone the 20 years since the flats' construction without being adhered to the concrete, is gone. She doesn't miss it. It stank of stale cigarette smoke. The reek was thanks to the previous occupiers. The fug of it seeps upwards after every spring clean. By June each year, the cuff of every sleeve, the dangling end of every scarf was steeped in the stench. She is glad that it's gone, she allows gladness to ramble over the quietly insistent question of where the offending floor covering could have disappeared to? She wouldn't have minded the sudden disappearance of the shitty lino, if not for the fact that the concrete floor beneath is also gone. Gone in a way that made the decision of where to stand rather complicated.

Shuffling to the doorframe, she plants her feet on the pine flooring of the hallway and leans as far into the dark as she dares. The thin bronze strip of a draft excluder is now a precipice. She sees nothing beyond the boundary but feels the dark extend. She feels it in the way a rodent senses the opening of space above her mousy head. Knows the vastness of human habitat once she leaves the confines of her tunnel through the skirting. She feels the vast cavern of air extending up above her despite her inability to see the ceiling.

She is sure the void in place of her pantry has dimensions, boundaries. It must have. Everything does. But, those dimensions, where the dark begins and where it ends, such geometry is outside of her current capabilities. All she wants is soup. She is already warming the bread under the grill, just a little to crisp the crust the way she likes it, heated to better receive the butter.

Barefoot, with her toes touching the rapidly cooling metal of the draft exclusion strip, she waves her hand through the dense cool dark. She considers in that moment that the flat is nothing but an antechamber. A dull domestic entrance room built to proceed into whatever this space is.

Stepping back into the hallway, she closes the door carefully folding the overstocked coat hook on the back of the door so as not to trap a sleeve in the jamb. She assumes there must be some mistake, that she used the door incorrectly. Perhaps turned that handle in some way she hadn't considered before. Maybe she has broken the room? She wonders if it is possible to break an entire room. She concludes after more moments staring at the door to nothingness that all things can break.

She is aware that rooms disappearing are not normal occurrences. She has lived 28 years without a single incident of a vanishing room. Vanishing objects within rooms, sure. But not entire rooms. She considers whether a pantry can be called a room. She wonders if having a pantry made her and Graham posh? Noting that if so, they no longer had to worry about the burden of their privilege. It does not make her feel any better. Any darkness behind a closed-door had never gone so far as to swallow the walls and floor. She wonders whether that is something she should be thankful for. She wonders about the sensation of the room disappearing while she is inside.

Retreating to the living room. Still hungry but her idle inkling for soup or, maybe pasta is buried now under the growing fear that the nothingness behind the door might spread. She fears the hallway wouldn't be safe. She fears that nowhere is safe. To leave the flat would mean walking past the yawning dark. Coats and gloss painted plywood would be little protection. Then there was the front door itself.

The front door was newly fitted, solid oak, impermeable. She hated the new door. She hated it because Graham had called the fitters to put it in when she was out. She had come home to an alien front door. Her home was no longer her home. The new door had been installed without the glass panes that the older door had. The older door had glass panes reaching from the middle bar of letterbox to the arch of the frame. This door stood solid, irresolute, without a trace, no single reminder that a world lay on the other side of it.

Graham wanted them to change the design. Graham said the frosted glass was a 'glaring security risk'. She liked the glass. It meant that in the case of visitors, she could see the person on the other side of the door. Discern the familiar shape of a takeaway delivery guy from that of a murderer. She wonders what a murderer would look like through frosted glass.

The new door has no glass. No way to see what exists beyond its threshold. She considers for a moment that if she opens the door to escape the dark only to find more darkness. What would she do? She had no idea that the pantry had absented itself when she'd opened the door. Maybe, she thinks, maybe the hallway outside the flat is also gone, and she doesn't know.

She curls her legs underneath her, suddenly cold. She wants to talk to somebody, anybody. She reaches for the phone but finds herself unable to dial. The numbers and names are less of a problem than what she could possibly say.

'Morning Mum',
'I'm fine. Good. Yeah'
'Haven't eaten yet, no.'
'Why? Oh, nothing. Just the pantry. Is gone'

Graham wouldn't be any more receptive. He was always quick to tell her she was irrational. For Graham, every problem was caused by her being emotional. She hated it when he called her 'silly'. When he came home three hours late without answering his phone, she was 'overreacting'. When he says he will handle dinner, and she comes home to him playing computer games, her frustration is 'further complicating the situation'. He never outright called her crazy, she knew he didn't need to. Just the thought of trying to explain the void in the pantry to him made her feel crazy. She thinks for the first time in a long time maybe she is mad. Maybe this is what it feels like to lose your mind. She doesn't feel crazy. But, she thinks, maybe that is just how these things work.

The ligaments in her knees begin to set. The skin on her legs is bloodless from the compression. Cold as a corpse. Cold and stubbled as granddad's cheek. She really had meant to shave her legs. She remembers being held up to kiss him in his coffin. She was embarrassed as she rose that he would see under the frills of her dress. It's funny how you remember these things. She had only been 4 when he stopped living. She didn't know the point at which she could only remember him dead.

The acrid taint on the air meant her toast was burning. She felt it grow in volume until it tickled at the corners of her eyes and the back of her throat. She cannot shake the image of the dark behind the door. It roars. A sonorous rumble that drowns out the tinny wail of the smoke alarm. She wonders what would be worse, burning to death or falling through infinite nothing for eternity. There must have been keys in the door, a familiar rattle and shuffle of his entrance. She hears instead:

'Fucks sake babe!' Anger makes his voice high and rasping. A sort of frustrated whine. 'Trying to fucking kill yourself! Are you fucking mad? look at it.' He must be in the kitchen now, 'it's fucking charcoal. How could you be so careless?'

'Hello to you too, darling. How was your day? She replies. "The void has come to take us." She thinks, she says. 'No, really, I'm fine.'

She is undecided as to whether she is more insulted by the accusation of carelessness or the inane suggestion anyone would deliberately kill herself through the burning of toast. She uncurls from the sofa and stands stretching the feeling back into her legs as Graham thunders about opening windows and wafting smoke.

'Are you *trying* to burn the flat down... eh? With your bloody toast?'

'I forgot; I was sort of dealing with…'

'With what? Straightening your hair or something? You can't just start cooking and forget it Meghan we've talked about this.'

'When have we "talked about this" Graham?' Another knife in his arsenal, every problem he had with her was endemic. A recurring cancer of an issue, however small. A pattern of behaviour even at its first instance.

'You do this all the time for fucks sake, 'his usual reply. 'You forget things, you're careless.'

She decides, upon consideration that burning to death would be preferable to infinite falling through space. She reasons eventually that the intense heat would crisp all nerve endings to the point of unresponsiveness. After all, piles of charred bone feel nothing. Falling, on the other hand, was never lethal. It was the stopping at the end that got you. Falling ceaselessly, she decided, was just another way of starving to death then desiccating in the cold emptiness at the end of all things. She wasn't about that.

She wonders if she had concluded earlier that a fiery end was better than an endless descent into the dark, she would have stayed with Graham after the work party. Whether she would have pressed on instead of folding when she confronted him about his work 'friend'. If she would have accepted the: "placing-my-hand-on-thearse-of-Claire-from-marketing-during-half-an-hourof-conversation-that-was-really-just-five-minutesyou-are-massively-exaggerating-and-no-peo-pledidn't-know-you-were-my-girlfriend-because-YOUdidn't-in-troduce-yourself-and-besides-we-areclose-its-just-what-friends-do-and-you'd-know-ifyou-had-any-male-friends" excuse he had machinegunned at her until she fell silent. Better to explode than fade, she thinks.

Graham is still wafting and swearing, she wonders why Graham can't take his wafting and swearing nearer to the actual smoke alarm that is still wailing. Its strangled meeps piercing even the cold stillness of her torpor. She wishes the alarm would go away. She wishes Graham with his stomping and his swearing and his judgment would just go away. She wishes she wasn't even here. She considers for a single tick of her watch that she, in fact, isn't here. That she, Megan, has left somehow, probably without letting herself know she was going out. That feeling is further compounded by Graham storming past to open yet another window, compounding the cold without paying her the slightest mind.

He doesn't see me, she thinks. But then again, he's never seen her. Because she is now invisible, she decides she should also remain silent. She thinks it only appropriate for those who go unseen to also go unheard.

So as Graham finally thinks to press the reset button and silence the alarm, she says nothing. As he grumbles his expletive-laden resentment into a struggle with his left shoe, she stays quiet. It's only when she hears him shrugging off his coat that she thinks it might be best to speak to him about the missing pantry. She thinks of the words she would use to explain the gaping hole in space that used to be where they kept the cardigans and tinned tomatoes. She follows him to the hallway

'Be careful babe the…'

'Me? Be careful? From the woman who I have to stop burning the flat down when she forgets her toast, or fucking curling iron or whatever.'

'I don't have a curling iron Graham, and the straightener was warming up when you unplugged it. You always fucking do this, Graham.' He reaches for the handle. 'you never ask, you just do. And it's never your fault is it? You turn off my straighteners, push me out the door complaining about being late, then bitch all night about how my hair got in your face when we sat next to each other...'

'I don't appreciate the Tone Megs, I really don't.' He's still looking at her, *now* of all moments he's looking at her. The dark is open now, a foot and a half of dark between the door frame and coat rack. His coat is half off his shoulder. His left hand is on the inside door handle. He has his back to nothingness. And now, he is looking at her.

'Because you refuse to take responsibility for anything, I have to just lie down and stay quiet? Is that it?' He just. Keeps. Going. 'Why are you so sensitive? I could deal with the fuck ups if you just owned them, but no, it *can't* be your fault, can it? You can never just be wrong; you have to sulk and pout like a....'

It was piercing, fearful and full-throated scream. Yet, it seemed to recede into silence almost as soon as it had come tearing into existence. After a few seconds, all she can hear is the quiet thrumming of empty space.

She notices the chill, not so much a draught but a slowly flowing surge of the air around her being displaced. She looks over the edge of nothing. The coat hook that had strained for so long against its perfunctory attachment by mismatched screws had been torn away. It, along with most of the winter coats, was gone.

After a while, she gathers the remaining cardigans and hats, strewn as shrapnel across the hallway floor. She fishes a scarf trailing out into the dark and closes the door to nothingness. She remembers the fridge holds half a roast chicken from last night. She decides reheated chicken would be superior to the soup. She tips the carbonite slab under the cooling grill into the bin. Better to burn than fade to nothing she thinks, realising Graham never really deserved 'better'. She knows that Graham would have never believed her anyway. She wonders at which point she will only remember him as dead.

The End of *Us*

The Couple

Sat across from us, the Couple have been a shining fixture in our dining experience for weeks. Though not quite across from us today, instead three tables away from us & two across. Everyone has noticed.

The couple draw the eye in ways only beings built for each other can. A meeting of split teak whorl for whorl & tanned. Good God they're tanned, the Couple, bronze & happy with a joy that ripples into the others around them as bitterness.

Women pull tight arm folds beneath pits; men suck in paunches pale as mold furred moons & the couple, smiling in their joy, teeth eye ache bright as northern European skies & so tall, She at least 6 foot & Him eye height with the waiter while sat & they're eating

the same all-inclusive buffet delicacies as everyone about them. Yet, in combinations that seem to be the only combinations that make any sense. Everything they eat, the couple, is something I want. They make me…

The Couple makes me salivate for Quinoa, this couple are eating Quinoa & though I have no fond memories, exactly of the taste of Quinoa, yet, as the couple eat it, I need it, we need it, we watch the couple with their ochre bodies eating Quinoa.

& we, the diners, heap the Quinoa onto ice cream, stir it into pints of warm larger, dust the sauce of Duck Chow Mein with the Quinoa & it is delicious. the Couple, the beautiful Couple, both so tall, 9-foot-tall, eyes the hues of split jade & the last oak in oxford, are laughing.

& their laughter is music & the diners cannot help but move to the music. They hate the couple with a love that exhibits itself first as disregard, strained neck muscle & furtive glances, lusty glimpses at a flash of Breast & rippling Back & Lips & Jaw.

Each diner would subsume themselves into that Back, those Breasts, if they could & many do, rising quietly, folding napkins tucking phones into pockets of Bermuda shorts & pressing themselves into the taught calves, the ebony flesh of the couple, so tall, so tanned, & they are consumed.

& the couple, two stories tall now obsidian & shining, they rise & as they rise, they sweep the dining room towards them with the gravity of a dying star & Quinoa streams in sandstorms off plates into their orbit & they tip the waiter with gold & they embrace.

& in their embrace is the world & the beauty of their embrace is like the oceans of the world & diners, some of them overcome by the embrace, begin to weep & strip off bootleg Arsenal jerseys, floral print sarongs. Baring their nakedness to the ocean of their joy, others overwhelmed, simply cease.

Exiting this place with a wistful sigh, leaving their fruit juice & skirt steak to the flies & the couple, their towering magnificence rendering the building to ruin, stride through the wreckage of the dining hall. & the diners, from the rubble, watch them stride.

Across the compound, palms blooming in the cool shadow of their passing, they step over the beach entire hand in hand into the ocean, dark & twinkling eyes blue shifted into the troposphere. Perfect fucking hair, in infinitely tessellating curls. The Couple hand in hand stride into the sea their footsteps quiver the cliffs & turn the sand to glass &
they are beautiful &
they are radiant &
they are gone.

64,800: 1

a slender arc of focus / a line of force / cancelling & cutting through the peripheral clutter of packed pub / I came here with you & after all these years we still move together / a seated dance / my hand to my earlobe follows yours/ perhaps in bonding / deep brain reflex / or because I cannot help but wonder / what that centimetre of skin feels like under my fingertips / at that precise second / despite me imagining / every other inch / at every other minute / years later I'm still intrigued by that *now* / by us there *then* / I'm looking up / from my book for the first time in two hours & so are you / & so the flow / of thought feels better / unbroken by contact / as if we'd lose the charge / dissipate the heady static / the gravity that draws my eyes to yours / this second of entangled glance / a fragment of mirror recognition / amongst the sixty four thousand / eight hundred of the day / we have been in orbit of each other but this / this moment of connection / shouldn't be much / no rational reasoning / makes it any more or less / worthy than any other moment / yet
dear God...

It's beautiful.

Mutually Assured Destruction

time and again	ǝʌol ɥʇᴉʍ ʇnɐʇ
we come to this	sᴉ ʇɥƃnɐɹɟ puɐ pᴉƃᴉɹɟ
all but spent	ssǝullᴉʇs ǝɥʇ
worn from the ruck	ǝɹns
still raging	'ʇᴉ pᴉɐs ǝʍ uǝɥʍ
long after we're	pᴉɐs ǝʍ ʇɐɥʍ
sure	uɐǝɯ ʇ,upᴉp
both of us	sn ɟo ɥʇoq
didn't mean	ǝɹns
what we said	ǝɹ,ǝʍ ɹǝʇɟɐ ƃuol
when we said it,	ƃuᴉƃɐɹ llᴉʇs
sure	ʞɔnɹ ǝɥʇ ɯoɹɟ uɹoʍ
the stillness	ʇuǝds ʇnq llɐ
frigid and fraught is	sᴉɥʇ oʇ ǝɯoɔ ǝʍ
taut with love	uᴉɐƃɐ puɐ ǝɯᴉʇ

Crown

for 2020

*

Remains, our gleaming trophy from its maw.
It doesn't feel like much, it's what we've got.
& from such gore we try to build a future
lace caps blooming fractal from the rot.
we should not hurry in our mourning
to salve the ache with liquor & with haste
there may not have been but five at any burial
but loss is sipped to stem the bitter taste.
If I could say a prayer, for you I'd pray.
If God in all her loving had not turned
to other worlds more deserving I would
say to her that her mercy is deserved
for you & all that sickness has forsworn.
Breathe deep, draw in a wide & open roar.

*

Breathe deep, draw in a wide & open roar!
unclench your jaw, part molars, space your grin.
exhale, release your hold on being in
that moment you existed, nothing more.
Be deep, be wide, be open if you can.
separate yourself from 'self' the art
is making all your being quiet & thin.
Present in the quaking, shifting start.
You draw a line, behind it is your past.
You make a mark, decide to make it now.
You carve a sweep, a scoring, straight & fast
& once it's made you step beyond it. This
is the first moment of your future. [AHHHH],
Was that the ragged breath of your dead past?

*

Was that the ragged breath of your dead past?
the prison that you carried, all its weight.
compressing vertebrae, eroding casque
as you exhaled, did you yet feel the hate?
the burden bearing down, that clammy fear
& did you shift the pressure or draw near
the virtue of your unassailable state
the world cries out for change & so you change.
Your lungs struggle for breath, so you inhale.
But did you shift your form to become more?
& is that 'more' great terror, warped & strange?
the pupae bring the butterfly we know,
yet also from such shells do hornets grow.

*

Yet also from such shells do hornets grow.
we watch them swarm & conquer in HD
struck by the rising numbers. Could we know
how vast the scale of terror? It must be
the kind of fear that conquers every sense
that roots you to the earth as you look on.
A crown that all could wear bestowing death.
It's finery a fevered racking cough,
that in that time between the errant breath
& the ventilator beep we could fight off.
Whatever plague dread formed that fills the place
of anapaests & synonyms. I'm numb
to death in ways, I'd thought I'd clambered past.
The year has taken all that it could grasp.

*

The year has taken all that it could grasp.
It's hunger devoured hope in hearty gulps
swallowing sense of self & we've become
accustomed to the fug of fattened hours.
It turned to time itself and bared its teeth.
we've lost, amongst the objects in the flood of
of massing minutes tearing pal-mal, out,
out, away from everything, from themselves,
the grasp on human motion without fear.
The sense of breathing unconsidered, free.
If breath itself had not become an effort,
the joy of living from a struggled waking
the binding knot of fear would act to choke
I lost myself beneath its titan's yoke.

Ω

I'd fight the host. I'd take a swing at God
I'll walk this void, face purgatory alone.
No self to give, no text, have all I've got.
If either sacrilege would keep you home
Instead, I learned how you forget yourself
I'd lost my reflection, nothing remained
pressed flat beneath the pale crown foetid wealth,
that any peace with death we'd made was feigned.
I lost myself beneath its Titans yoke.
The year has taken all that it could grasp.
'Yet also from such shells do hornets grow.'
Was the last ragged breath of your dead past.
Breathe deep, draw in a wide & open roar?
Remains, our gleaming trophy from its maw.

*

I lost myself beneath its Titans yoke.
I'll admit, I thought myself annealed
to panic at 'the end'. The cosmic joke
that is my body of burned glass, healed
just enough to take another breaking.
made me used to hanging on, I thought
made me calm confronting that deep quiet.
I thought. I mind sickness much more than death.
In this year, when the blight reached out to us
pale king of ventilator hiss and huff
its crown taught me the lie of my misgiving
that first, I would be unbowed to its reign
& second, as its weight pressed out my breath
any peace with death we'd made was feigned.

*

Any peace we'd made with death was feigned.
We felt that was the lesson, our great learning.
Laying in the glistening still, blissed but pained
our bodies still not fit to match our yearning
"I know it's not" you say, "It couldn't be,
but it feels like *a* first time" I reply
"almost as good" & hope you cannot see
my grimace in the dark, my struggling sigh
my grappling with the memory of us
before the tear of this came through our home
& stripped me back to promises & dust.
"Almost" you speak to sleep, then I'm alone
gasping dark, dry drowning in failing health.
pressed flat beneath the pale crowns foetid wealth.

*

Pressed flat beneath the pale crowns foetid wealth.
I crawled to see what thing I had become
& found that in the mirror stood a feat
of mimicry, so strange it struck me dumb.
There, standing in the frame stood a black man
the very image of my former self
except where I would move, he would just stand
I could not make him do anything else.
I wandered in a stupor to the sink
to splash or retch I did not know, maybe a
drink of something, cold would help me think
when a white shimmer in the water glowed
the bathroom light beyond my head showed plain.
I'd lost my reflection, nothing remained.

*

I'd lost my reflection, nothing remained.
So, this is what it was to become new?
To draw a line, to burn the bridge, to see
nothing but the future that might be
& find that future grins without face.
To find yourself amongst those made to reign.
To bargain with Osiris for deliverance
then find yourself returned a fragile wraith.
I sat up in the half light of a dawn
knowing that deleting what I'd been when
the world had nothing for me to make new
meant timeless waste & sickness lay before me.
Resolved to quit the past, forgive myself.
Instead, I learned how you forget yourself.

*

Instead, I learned how you forget yourself.
In searching for a way to be made free
I needed to be better & this year
was my year. God, we needed it to be.
The burdens that we'd carried to this summit.
the plans we'd made, the sacrifices, scars,
the tender tissues holding us together,
to be torn apart by shifting in the stars?
By dice rolls in the cosmic? By small men
hiding failure, playing God? You are the
stone of my foundation. You're the point
upon which my galaxy wheeled. I'd rip
the sacred pen & wings from Metatron
If either sacrilege would keep you home.

*

If either sacrilege would keep you home
or sacrifice to some indolent Geist.
I'd make them & I said as much. Alone
we might just make it. But we've trod
the path of solitude & found that though
we bested every foe, the victories
were pyrrhic & the battle spoils hollow.
Relentlessly the lone survivors of
each wave of life assault, each cosmic blow.
Until we met & tackled them as one.
Back-to-back, we took on the world & won.
My body, like my mirror image fades.
I'm pinned between four walls & yawning loss.
No self to give, no text, have all I've got.

*

No self to give, no text, have all I've got
I give it freely. If in some return
for such a paltry offering you give
me time, wait till I build myself again.
As Caliban was formed of clay & dream
I shall write myself a better body
pour libations that Ṣọpọna might see
the Sisyphean heft of daily plodding
these clotted lungs, these frayed neurons uphill.
This place is such a desolate Kingdom.
the land ordained for those of us who left
the healthy long enough to lose ourselves
then could not return, nor in death find home.
I'll walk this void, face purgatory alone.

I'll walk the void, face purgatory alone.
I'll take the kraken on with one held breath.
I'll restore old Jericho stone by stone.
With you here at my back I'll conquer death.
We'll break the crown & liberate the kingdom.
We'll build ourselves a safe and caring home.
We'll take each melee on, just as we used to
with me behind you, love you'll crush them all.
The world will shake when we make our arrival.
We'll pull this ruck apart & rout its spall
& once we've helped each other through this war
we'll be unstoppable, beyond all scorn.
Then to ensure all obstacles are gone
I'd fight the host. I'd take a swing at God.

Leave to Remain

I am not sure if
this is a poem
or a dream

nonetheless I say crack
the window love for
we invite the dark

listen we are travellers here
only ever visitors to night
leave as you find

we do not belong
lacking the appropriate
papers to stay

till morning would make us
criminals nonetheless
we crack knuckles

in the dark
memorised parables
in preparation

for war I say split
when they come for us
& we'll try to –

nonetheless, you sit
in silence thinking of loss
pondering probability

the rhythm of footsteps
disposition for quiet
coalescing outside the door

unsure of the nature of
our endings yet knowing
they end, we wait.

Oblivion Hymn #2

The tea has cooled to blood
temperature & the flannel warmed
to blood temperature. Bissi, fennel
& mint for sweetness, ginger
to settle rebellious viscera, I
hurt too much to hold, Darling
does the coat of thorns face in?
Or curve cruel out? If I take
myself away would you help
me leave? My Love
where would we go?

Close to you
-A film

INT. LIVING ROOM - EVENING

MIKE and CHARLIE sit almost motionless at opposite ends of
the sofa in a darkened living room. Curtains drawn to the low
evening sun. Faces illuminated by the glow of the television
screen.

Mike, 28, Wiry with close cropped dark hair, tense with
persistent arrested inertia, in this moment hair triggered but
trying not to show it. A face with the capacity to hold a
magnificent smile that has fallen out of use. And Charlie 32,
Compact and leonine, his head crowned with short dark gold
curls that pick up and carry the colours of the screens radiance.
Wide bright eyes that can harden to flint in seconds. They are
granite now.

Static tension saturates the Living room. Low audio of vapid
regional soap opera permeates just loud enough to hear but not
loud enough to cover a...

Mike & Charlie
(Sigh loudly)

Simultaneous and frustrated. Both watchers desperate to
change the channel. Charlie allows a glimmer of a smile, Mike
shifts in his seat. The couple glance at each other for barely a
second. Then. They harden again, continuing to glare at the
screen unmoving.

The remote control sits in the empty void of plush seating
between them. A black rectangle stark against biscuit velvet that
bounces the colour of the TV Strobing, green, blue, pink then
golden. The couple behave forcibly oblivious of each other,
avoiding eye contact, touch, making personal space electrified
barrier. Neither welcoming of each other's company nor yearn-
ing to be alone.

The remote control waits, still. Mike flicks his eyes to the right, glances down at the control then at the stone-faced Charlie. then back to the TV.

Charlie doesn't want to end the stalemate, choosing to resume his feigned watching unwilling to give Mike something to argue about.

Mike shifts in his seat. Gets up, leaves to go to the kitchen. through an open arch in the living room wall opposite the window.

Charlie ignores his passing, then a moment after he leaves, dives for the remote. Pressing a button, any button. The program changes. Soft music, the screen glows red.

INT. KITCHEN - EVENING

Mike stands in the kitchen listless. Unsure why he is even in the room he goes first to the fridge. Gazing in passively as if the cold light were an open window to a grey day. Then to the kettle. It's already full but as he reaches to press the switch he hesitates.

> Mike
> (Under breath)
> Fucks-sake...what's the point. Just gonna
> get a mouthful...

His frustration rising, he oscillates between walking away and making the cup of tea he wants, before rolling his eyes, he bellows.

> Mike (cont'd)
> Fancy a tea?

INT. LIVING ROOM - EVENING

Charlie Starts, flustered at the shout that broke the silence. before he can stop himself. he spits.

Charlie
So, we're using whole words now?

Mike
'fucksake Charles, I want tea, not a
scrap. Do you want tea?

Charlie
Blanked me for the best part of two
days. Now you want to make me tea.

Mike
Forget it.

Charlie
Which bit Michael? The, 'We need to
talk' that petered out into just…
whatever the fuck this is?

The kettle begins to boil in the adjoining kitchen and His
frustration rises with the rising roil of bubbles.

Charlie (cont'd)
Or that you are leaving the *fucking*
country in 2 weeks and didn't think it
was worth mentioning to…

He stops short as Mike comes back into the room with a mug of
tea and a sandwich. Balancing the plate on the arm of the sofa he
sips his tea then casually sits in his usual spot. Silence ensues.

Charlie
The fuck is wrong with you?

Mike explodes. In one deft move he swipes the plate and
sandwich to the floor. Picks up his tea and strides into the
kitchen. The plate bounces but does not break. Bread, cheese,
and lettuce splatter across the carpet.

                    Charlie (cont'd)
          Oh! So, he experiences *emotion*. Its
          ALIVE!

                         Mike

          Fuck off!

Mike rounds the corner to the kitchen. Still fuming he throws
his full mug into the sink, Scalding tea splashes up his arms, he
wrestles himself back into shape, struggling into composure.
Grabs a towel, dries tea of his arms turning again, to storm back
into the living room and unload on Charlie

                         Mike
          I can't fucking talk to! —

INT. LIVING ROOM -DAY

Sunlight streams through the windows, curtains open. Stopping
him in his tracks. The carpet is clear, the sofa empty. Mike stands
in the living room dazed as there's a chatter of keys at the front
door. Which opens to Charlie, eyes dark, looking worn, but
dressed for work. He drops his keys and wallet next to the tele-
vision, then notices Mike, he stands stock still, frustration relief
and rage flickering over his face.

                        Charlie
          Where the HELL have you been
          Michael?

                         Mike

          Whu-?

                        Charlie
          It's been 2 fucking days. You smash
          about the kitchen. Then you just leave.
          Saying nothing. I waited up all night —

                         Mike
          What are you on about? Not being
          funny-

Charlie

Oh... funny? yeah. Funny how you told
me to *FUCK OFF* and then *you* left,
then as usual we *must* pretend nothing
happened at all! All is right with Mike.
No harm no foul, water under the
fucking—

Mike

I was just in the—

Charlie

My god, did you go out in your fucking
Joggers and Flip flops? You're wearing
the same clothes as you were Saturday,
I called your phone Mike. For 2 hours
straight, over, and over. Text you like
twenty times. Before I found it charging
next you your wallet and keys in the
bedroom.

Mike

Why are you? -

Charlie

Then I really worried. God, I worried
Mike. I'm Losing my fucking mind
thinking who goes out without their
phone for hours on end. I thought
about ringing hospitals, as if that's even
a thing you can do—

Mike begins to pace before the archway to the kitchen, arms
crossed behind his head. The tea towel flapping behind him. His
face wrought with the effort of piecing together the fractured
Logic of his past 10 minutes.

Mike

Babe... I Just —

Charlie

Called the non-emergency number, I
hung up, I called again, hung up. Cause
what the fuck was I supposed to say to
them? 'Hi, my Boyfriend who is acting
like a stranger and just booked a flight
out of the fucking country without
telling me after 4 years of living
together, just threw a sandwich across
the room and walked into the night in
his damn slippers?'

Mike

Charlie, love I—

Charlie

'Why, *no,* officer, he didn't throw the
sandwich *at me,* no, that would have
been an *emotional response*, and you
see my boyfriend, my love, isn't fucking
capable of expressing emotion—

Mike

Okay, what are you? —

Charlie

At least I didn't think so until he upped
and left. But then again, I didn't know
he was flying one way to FUCKING
Germany, officer, so maybe I didn't
know him that well at all.

Mike

Can you just let me —

Charlie

YOU SHUT UP. Shut the hell up and
listen…I even called Luke to see if you'd
gone to his. Haven't seen or
spoken to them in a year Mike, they

weren't exactly at the top of my list, but
I couldn't think of where the fuck else
you'd go to on foot without your wallet
or phone or even a coat. And you know
what? fucking Clara picked up and you
KNOW I can't stand-

Mike
-I was in the KITCHEN... I've been
right

Charlie
If it wasn't enough to have me cutting
myself on shards of mug trying to un-
block the sink.

Charlie raises His left hand, a plaster wraps around the palm
from the first knuckle of his little finger to the heel of his thumb.
Mike turns to look at the sink, it's clear now. There's a pin prick
spatter of dark blood on the splash back that wasn't there before.
His confusion turning into a faint queasiness.

Charlie. cont.
You *Dick*. You could have jumped off
a fucking bridge Mike. You could have
been dead. It's been two whole days. I
didn't know... You made me think you
were DEAD. What *the actual* fuck?

Charlie tears up, fighting sobs, though from frustration or relief
it's impossible to discern. Mike realises he needs to bring this
situation back down, something is wrong, he's not sure what but
his lover is hurting. He adopts a conciliatory tone. Palms raised,
holding the towel like a white flag.

Mike
Look, I'm not sure what's happening
here. I don't know why you're dressed
for... when it's like 7 in the...

Mike glances at the wall clock. It reads 1:20 and as he stares it ticks its way to 1:21.

                    Mike. cont.
            The…fuck?

                    Charlie
            What?... WHAT? What could you
            possibly come out with that would even
            go a fraction of the way towards
            answering for this?

                    Mike
            I… I just. I was in the kitchen…I

                    Charlie
            [a beat, then quietly]
            Seriously… fuck you Michael.

Charlie turns and walks away; we hear him make his way up the stairs. A door clicks shut. Charlie stands in the daylight of the living room.

INT. BEDROOM - DAY

Charlie paces about the bedroom, grim in angry silence.
The muffled tap of each step. Accompanies the furious unbuttoning of his shirt. He stops only to take an identical fresh one from the drawer. The sound of Mike's socked feet coming up the stairs along the landing stop behind the closed door.

                    Mike
            I'm Sorry babe. I'm not sure what's
            going on. It's all a bit…

                    Charlie
            Why won't you talk to me? We don't
            talk about things anymore. Not real
            things.

There is silence, beyond the door, nothing but presence. But he feels Mike there. He moves close enough to kiss the frame. he hesitates.

> Charlie
>
> Do you remember when we used to make up through the door...At one point I felt we only said what we really felt with a couple inches of pine between us. [pause] I'm sorry... It's just how I feel. I can't trust you. You were going to just leave? After years. It's not something I can just let go... And you just...You just refuse to talk about it so... Mike?

More silence, this time oppressive.

> Charlie (to himself)
> And you don't wanna' talk about it now.

He quietly walks over to the wardrobe, takes out a large weekend bag. Then to the drawers. Folding each item delicately before placing them in the bag. A gentle contrast to the frustrated bustle of before. Beginning to pack he speaks aloud.

> Charlie
>
> I'm going to go to dads for a... few days... I'll head back to the office and drive up this evening... I'm sorry. Mike? you there?

Folding stops.

> Charlie
>
> Mike?

He strides to the door. Pulling it open to a darkened hallway. Directly outside the door a crowbar, hammer, and drill with a broken bit litter the floor. The walls about him pulse with striated shadows cast by the glow of late-night TV bouncing through the banister rails. Each beam hangs in the suddenly dense, stale air. He pads down the steps. The house is warm and dark and unfamiliar. At the foot of the stairs, he stumbles. The clatter of cardboard and cans, as illuminated in the reflective haze a line of black bags snakes from the stairs to the front door. Bolted and chained from the inside.

> Charlie
> (softly)

Mike?

INT. LIVING ROOM - NIGHT

> Mike
> In here... babe?... you've gotta come in
> here.

> Charlie
> I don't... I can't see you.

> Mike
> I'm on the sofa. Just please? Come in
> here.

He steps over the black bags and through the door frame. Looking around a living room littered with plates and mugs. Some still smeared with remnants of meals others in active states of decay. Speechless, Mike is tense and afraid, Holding his breath.

Charlie steps over the threshold, as he approaches the sofa Mike relaxes.

The man looking up at him from the sofa is barely recognisable. Flickering wildly in the glow of a TV on mute. A thicket of beard, hair the awkward length only a long-delayed haircut can bring, no edges, beginning to matt, his skin dull and slightly sallow. The couple simply consider each other.

                    Mike (cont'd)
I couldn't figure it out at first. You went
upstairs. And we were talking. And
then I was telling you about Munich
and then I couldn't hear you anymore.
You'd locked the door, or blocked it or
something, 'cause I couldn't get it open.
So, I just left it. But when I wanted to
go to bed the door was still- I put the
bolt on the door. I'm sorry, I know I'm
a hypocrite, but I was scared you would
leave. and I needed to... I know I can't
really complain that you were doing to
me what-anyway... I um... slept on the
clothes in the spare room. Brought you
coffee in the morning. But you wouldn't
come out. Later on... I was so pissed.
I just lost it. I tried to break the door
down, but it wouldn't budge. It was like
a wall... not even wood.

                    Charlie
I don't und-
                    Mike
I think... it's been. You were upstairs for
three weeks Charlie.

                    Charlie
Babe, what's Happ-

                    Mike
It's all gone off, I thought I was losing it.
I didn't know what to do.

EXT. House DAY

A distressed Mike stands outside their house. The front door is
open. He is at the end of the path. Looking up to a bedroom win-
dow that seems to be glowing grey. He makes his way to the drain-
pipe and begins awkwardly trying to climb. The plastic creaking

                    Mike (VO)
          I tried climbing in from the outside.
          You know? Like when we came back
          from new years and your key snapped
          in the lock and you really needed the
          loo? the window was open, you like the
          air. so, I went up except the bedroom.
          Through the window was just blank.

Mike peers through the window into a pale nothingness.
Permeated by indistinct shapes.

                    Mike (VO)
          The curtains were open, but it was
          just. The light. The light was all wrong.
          when I came in my watch was wrong
          the evening news was on, but I climbed
          up before midday... I... When I went
          to the kitchen that night. Remember?
          When I disappeared? Well, I was in
          the kitchen. I never left. I smashed my
          mug, I'm sorry. I was raging. I turned
          around to have a go and it was day.
          Suddenly day. I'm thinking when I lost
          sight of you... somehow you went on
          living without me.

Mike clears his throat, swallowing hard and dry. Crushing fatigue and the need to talk after so long, battle it out behind a thin quivering smile.

INT. HALLWAY - EVENING (FLASHBACK)

Mike sits at the top of the stairs. looking from the door to the bedroom, down into the rest of the house then off into space. He is splintering, becoming more desperate. He gets up and hammers on the door calling out to Charlie, but we hear nothing but the narration of his ordeal.

                    (V.O. Mike)
            I don't blame you. It happens, allegedly.
            It happens. It kept happening to me. I
            knew you hadn't gone. I sat watching
            the front door for a day and a half.
            when I noticed there was no sunset. or
            streetlamps. The light was wrong
            outside. I couldn't go out. I was sure
            Laura would call from the office
            eventually. I hadn't been to work I
            started thinking, it had something to do
            with distance. Not miles and stuff but.
            Us. If I focussed on something other
            than you, the days would just... our
            distance and…

INT. LIVING ROOM -?

Mike sits up, straightening his spine with a stiff crackle, agitat-
ed. He has run this story over a hundred times. but to say these
thoughts out loud?

                        Mike
            I started thinking. What if it happened
            to you? What if I was the one to carry
            on living, leaving you hours, or days
            behind. And I just couldn't do it. So, I
            waited. And the wrong light it kept…
            its everywhere.

Mike gestures to the bay window, Charlie looks, the curtains are
partially closed. His eyes adjusting, we can see beyond them
there is nothing. A flat grey glow. Light suffused emptiness.
Stunned into silence, Charlie stands staring, for a moment he
is reeling. We see the sliver of bright emptiness reflected in the
curve of his eyes glistening in close up. We hear the light now
and realise we've been hearing it all along. it is TV static. It is the
hum of florescent tubes. The persistent white noise of all on the
peripheries of perception but now… no longer peripheral.

Charlie sweeps the middle sofa cushion free of crisp packets crumbs and debris and sits down next to Mike.

Charlie

I'm not gonna...I don't understand
what happening. I'm not gonna pretend
I do. But I need you to know what ever
is happening I'm not going anywhere.
I'm staying right here with you. If you
want to get out of here, get on a plane
whatever I'm coming too. I'm not
leaving you love.

Mike

Frankfurt...I was just gonna Go,

Charlie

What?

Mike

I'm sorry. For an interview at first. The
European office then things started to
fall apart, and it just felt easier to go. I
felt crushed by all this. By everything.
I thought that it would hurt less, like a
clean break, ripping off a plaster or... I
don't know. We were just coasting. We
were fucking unhappy and love wasn't
enough was it? So I was just going to
leave.

Charlie

Why are you telling me this now?

Mike

Because I don't want the last words
between us to be lies.

Charlie Notices that the even glow of nothing has increased in intensity, the room has been getting steadily brighter. He turns to the doorway into the living room. There is nothing beyond the frame but light. The two men sit together looking into the

blankness. Mike quietly begins to weep. Simply allowing the
tears to come.

                    Mike
          Not sure exactly what I broke, but I
          don't think we have much of a choice
          now. I didn't think that. us,   we… you
          know… would break *everything*.

                    Charlie
                (turns to Mike)
          You were my everything.

                    Mike
          [beat] Oh.

                FADE TO WHITE

The End of the *World*

Countrycide

We are not dying.   No.

The cox rot   on heavy boughs fecund rumps
of melon squash   black with flies
& tubers treasured   since the blight   of black four
seven   seed & split   take their chance
in the loam   to be mothers too young.

Badger trundles   from her burrow
butts her hoary head   to the twin barrels
of the cull.   This year
there are no longer cows, the cows   are gone.
Where   more than three elm   stand to-
gether   two are aflame.   The high street
 littered with   acorns mouldering.

A white   van in a lake   settles in the sludge.   We
ignore the frantic   scratch beyond the doors.
We have manners   this   is England.

These days,   the waves   are ruled
by a mothballed carrier   in the Tyne
these days,   Britannia hurls   her spear
into the open   dark

These days,   our coffins   are *English* oak.
These days,   we speak   *English*   in the kebab
shop   *English*   You mug.   Speak it.
These days   are not your days   anymore.
What are you staring at? Got a problem?   Don't look
at me.   Don't *fucking*   look at me.

Brother, where lies your white city?

But postmodern theories of text and analysis have long since become commonplace in the discourse both of the academy and wider culture, and perhaps the *truly* radical now would be to see a deep political shift from the left to the right, or the substitution of a committed neo-Georgian ruralism for a (de)constructivist urbanism in the halls of innovative poetics. The fact that such unbreakable taboos exist reveals the limited aspirations of the so-called radicalism of the recent avant-garde, if, by that, we mean an art which might genuinely shake itself, and, as a consequence, us.

> - Toby Martinez De las Rivas: 'Conflict and Change in the Poetic Theologies of C.H. Sisson and Jack Clemo', PN Review, issue 217   (May-June 2014):

I didn't, in fact, come to learn of its existence as a symbol associated with Nazism until much more recently. The association seemed to me—and still seems to me—highly tenuous and amounts to one symbol at Wewelsburg castle which seems to have held no particular significance to the Nazis; in fact, it was not called a "black sun" until 1991, according to Wikipedia. This isn't ideal, but I trusted the critical engagement of my readership and proceeded. No allusion to the Wewelsburg symbol was at any time intended.

> - A Response: Toby Martinez De las Rivas on Black Sun & Titan/All is still, *Poetry Magazine* 2018.

Brother, where lies your white city?
-After 'Titan/All is Still' by Toby Martinez De las Rivas

I heard you in mourning. Saw the rising
in the west obliterate & render
mute the union. I tasted it. The
ache in the wet of your text, your anguish
as you implored Hím. '*Father*,' Hill & hart
were countenance to our raucous descent.
We, Golgothites looked upon a Titan.
Crucified, serenading the shrouded
past with a rhythm falling, as a
death march. We saw no funerals, only
bones. Your poem was a sky burial,
we saw no ritual through the meat. see

Brother,
   we know the black sun.
we see it needled to the shoulders of
'patriots' imagined pale riders.
We see it adorning silver trifles,
dainty upon the breasts of white women
smiling with all but their eyes as they lie
to millions of watching eyes, assert
with polite eloquence & assured guile
that 'pride is a *right*; *they* will not replace *us*.'
We see ourselves rendered in its dark light
From diaspora, to migrant other,
to those curséd, blighted, black sons of Ham.
This black sun you speak of over the west.
Rising as an omen, unfolding on
a bright blank Albion of fathers, your
fathers-fathers-fathers-fathers-fathers
whose hands wrapped calloused about sabre hilts,
whip handles, shackle keys, their hungry sons.
We few of the burning now see wild,
heinous symbols between the stars &
heavy dark. We, sown with the salt grit of
emptiness. We, knowing of coming war,

*"forever & ever
& his government will
never fail, for no glory/
is allowed but his glory, no
bone/ gouvernance but his
bone gouvernance,/
no prison camp but his
prison camp,/
his plantations, his will &
techne, his punishment/
beatings, his censorship,
his textual criticism, /
his forgiveness, his reha-
bilitation, O/ ferdful men,
& vnbileueful & cursid &
manquelleris."*

74

knowing we will taste it in our brief lives.
We, who know our enemy & their
cruelty & their history & seductive
glamour. We, who can never know when.
Your England,

Brother,
          is a *broken* land.
Shattered & shifting. Ambulant from moor
to ash crowned gorse, from Lullington church to
the golden windows of the last estate.
It lurches on, the corpse of an empire
& We? We uproarious censors
We eat the rot, the worm, the blight,
the pustulence, dark necessity.
We, detritivores, first to fall upon
the plague lamb. We, the hated shrieking in
the bone white sky, the excoriators.
Gnawing away the necrotic ideas
From the body we share, were we so wrong
to think you sustenance. You, speaking of
the state in tight hieroglyphs, the grave wrap
of ethnocrats? the thrice faded trappings
of tyrants? Were we not to hear the
language of scrubbed white marble, of
Wewelsburg stone, of the shields of 'fine men'
at Charlottesville, of the Sonnenrad,
of the Obergruppenführersaal &
seethe?

"You are the cast-away of drowned remorse/ You are the world's atonement on the hill. / This is your body twisted by our skill into a patience proper for redress. I cannot turn aside from what I do;/ you cannot turn away from what I am./ You do not dwell in me or I in you."

Brother,
          we heard your calling out
to the dead Lord in hís dead city &
thought, to our shame, you were supplicant to
the false law. The lie of blood and soil.
Greater for the myth of its extinction.
Your land, your longing, is as foreign to
us as dream. We speak but one language
via many scattered tongues & hearts.
Such hearts, beating in each of us. Struck once

For Heather Heyer, once for Joe Cox, once
for Ricky John Best, once more for Taliesin
Myrddin Namkai-Meche, a thrum Tattoo
for the Seventy-Seven of Utøya,
for the fifty-one poor souls of Christchurch
& more for Richard Collins III.
As struck your heart For Mame Mbaye.
Linked by sorrow and fibre optics
our chests beat ceaselessly for the ocean of
dead laid thick upon the land uncounted
by a charnel state, half steel/half chocolate
sweet as sunlight to those pure of master's
blood. The flood of bodies trickles to a
stream only as we rout the *Fäsh* & burn
their enclaves, yet daily we charge screaming
into smoke. We,
Brother,

        are losing grip. We're bleeding.
Amidst your love, your pastoral yearning.
We shook at the vision of a nation
state extending eternal, omnipresent
& clean (of us) blessed unto mouse &
mistook hér protection for a call
to our annihilation. Easily done. Yes?
Caught the ostentatious tolerance of
the popinjay in our dim reflection.
bridled at the thought that one could signal
virtue, that the beauty of the rot
was the truth we were blind to. Easily done.
      Brother,
           no love lost among young poets.
Ink before blood. Though spilling either
leaves a mark, neither painless, each a scar.
We move on to other battlefields.
Sing your song of personal extirpation
Choirs from Blake to Burzum sang as one.
They too saw cities prideful, concuipisant
in ways that history would know as love.
They too would hunger for a homeland lost
To them, to time, a land that never was.

*"Sed omnis una manet
nox et calcanda semel
via leti."*
*"But one-night waits for
all and the road of death
is to be tread only once."*

though now our pennants gutter in the half
heart wind that scours from the continent.
After travelling space, you travelled to profess,
be told brother, that the dark gods of
your pantheon are known by other names.
If *we* could read the horror of the black
sun rising? learn harsh histories in its glow.
hateful calls for bleak annihilation,
the siren song of tyranny & sorrow,
then You, brother with your passion for our
art, could have surely done the same?

Notes:

- "You are the castaway…" v.3-4 Lachrimae Verae, *Tenebrae*, Geoffrey
Hill.
- "Forever & ever…" Ln. 106-114. Titan/All is Still, *Black Sun*, Toby
Martinez De las Rivas
- "Sed omnis una manet…" -Carmina, *Liber I*, XXVIII

Ghazal For the Love of Nations.

Analysts have generally ignored these texts, as if poetry were a colourful but ultimately distracting by-product of jihad. But this is a mistake. It is impossible to understand jihadism—its objectives, its appeal for new recruits, and its durability—without examining its culture. This culture finds expression in a number of forms, including anthems and documentary videos, but poetry is its heart. And, unlike the videos of beheadings and burnings, which are made primarily for foreign consumption, poetry provides a window onto the movement talking to itself. It is in verse that militants most clearly articulate the fantasy life of jihad.

> - Robyn Creswell and Bernard Haykel: on Poetry flourishing amongst Daesh Jihadis in *Battle Line*. The New Yorker, 2015

Poetry has deep roots in Arabic culture and tradition, yet al-Nasr's poetry is not an expression of devotion to Islam, but rather the utilization of a cultural art form to make the personal identity of terrorists resonate with the wider public. Her meticulously crafted poetry shows the [Daesh] efforts to shift the image of jihadists from barbaric and savage archetypes to eloquent and intelligent individuals. This not only reflects the changing face of [Daesh] jihad, but gives the organization a seemingly unique angle, allowing them to easily reach out to the wider public and become closer to 'ordinary people.

> - Halla Diyab: *Ahlam al-Nasr: Islamic State's Jihadist Poetess* in Militant Leadership Monitor Volume: 6 Issue: 6 June 30, 2015.

Ghazal For the Love of Nations.

After 'The Blaze of Truth' by Ahlam Al- Nasr

Some amongst us write as if our nations weren't aflame.
We poets, as if our lives, our hopes were not aflame.

So few of us dare scar the flesh of page, they write platitudes.
So, few trace our anguish in calligraphic flame.

The citadel is breached, a virgin since the Ayyubid,
barrels burst on Hawl al Qalaa.st, the stones aflame.

A usurer stands before a billboard, foreign faces, dark & strained.
'They,' he lies 'are thieves & would-be-neighbours'. His crowd, inflamed.

Abn khabaz prostrates before a voice adjacent to the void.
Drives the car he practiced in towards the embassy, it ends in flame.

A baron's son on a bully pulpit drawls into a microphone
of letter boxes, picaninnies. My rage is cold, pale as flame

Sister Ahlam, we each looked out, five years ago & 2 hours apart.
& came to know. How could we write as if our nations weren't aflame?

Yet, you turned from flensing tyrants with your verses.
calling fire on Assad, awoke the world to Dara'a with your name,

to penning couplets in honour of defilers.
To embracing the behemoth, praising destroyers, without shame?

While I, I kept my silence I admit. Spoke little of atrocity. Hoping
between songs for my oppressor & the stake. I would choose flame.

Deteriorating Situation

-from the statement of Minister for the Middle East
Alistair Burt MP 14th May 2018.

*

"The violence today in Gaza and the West Bank has been shocking. The loss of life and the large number of injured Palestinians is tragic, and it is extremely worrying that the number of those killed continues to rise. Such violence is destructive to peace efforts. We have been clear that the UK supports the Palestinians' right to protest, but these protests must be peaceful. It is deplorable that extremist elements may have been seeking to exploit these protests for their own violent purposes. We will not waver from our support for Israel's right to defend its borders. But the large volume of live fire is extremely concerning. We continue to implore Israel to show greater restraint. The UK remains committed to a two-state solution with Jerusalem as a shared capital. All sides now need to show real leadership and courage, promote calm, refrain from inflaming tensions further, and show with renewed urgency that the path to a two-state solution is through negotiation and peace."

*

"The violence today in Gaza and the West Bank .
The loss of life and the large number of injured Palestinians ,
    is extremely worrying **that** the number of those killed
               is destructive   . We have been
clear that
                    ,
               . It is deplorable
         seeking to exploit these protests for   violent
purposes. We will not waver from our
      borders.
      . We continue to implore Israel to show   .

             .   leadership and
courage, promote calm, refrain from inflaming tensions further, and show
      negotiation   ."

*

*

"The violence today   .
The loss of life and the large number of injured
                              the number of those killed continues
to rise. Such violence is   peace   . We have been clear
that the UK supports   ,

                    .

                                                  their own violent
purposes. We will not waver from our support for
          borders.   live fire is extreme
          .   greater   .
The UK remains   a   state solution
a   capital.   real leadership
      ,   ,   inflaming tensions further,
      with renewed urgency
                              "
                              .

                    *

      . Such violence is   peace   . We have been clear
                                                ,
                    .   extremist elements
      seeking to exploit   violent
purposes. We will   support
                    .   the large volume of live fire
          . We continue to implore   .

      capital. All sides now
            ,   inflaming tensions further,
                    the path to a   solution is
through   peace."
                              *

Fire Hose

We are not optimistic about the effectiveness of traditional counterpropaganda efforts. Certainly, some effort must be made to point out falsehoods and inconsistencies, but the same psychological evidence that shows how falsehood and inconsistency gain traction also tells us that retractions and refutations are seldom effective. Especially after a significant amount of time has passed, people will have trouble recalling which information they have received is the disinformation and which is the truth. Put simply, our first suggestion is don't expect to counter the firehose of falsehood with the squirt gun of truth.

- Christopher Paul, Miriam Matthews: The Russian "Firehose of Falsehood" Propaganda Model, Why It Might Work and Options to Counter It, 2016

Fire Hose

- Verbatim: Donald J. Trump, Charlottesville press conference, Aug. 15, 2017.

Oblivion Hymn #3

Today, more people died
than when the first plane
hit the towers. In other
news, we have begun a
ritual of 8pm applause.

The Truth of the Earth

- Desig. C T S -

** Transcript of audio interview with detainee #78-607 Subject: VERRO
Pre-Collapse Dev: Commenced: 2.38PM CET, 15th August 1987 **

No… Yes, water is fine. My throat is. Thank you. Back to the beginning again? Or a different set this time? I can assure you the content of my responses will be no…

[Interrogator question [redacted] 5 seconds]

No list today then. Just a conversation. I appreciate the attempt at civility.

[Interrogator question [redacted] 27 seconds]

We are back on the old world, are we? It was said that Khrushchev lacked much of the ideological fervour that Stalin had so particularly embodied as the second father of our nation. But those amongst the politburo that whispered such claims were diffidently misinformed. It was by Khrushchev's direct request, or so we were informed, that we at laboratory 19 shifted our research from preventing the fungal blight that was decimating much of the corn crop each year to isolating and studying it.

[Interrogator question [redacted] 17 seconds]

No… though I'm surprised at the impertinence of the question. You Americans were well known to be flailing in your attempts to weaponize the cordyceps fungus. What horrors you could have unleashed if you had succeeded in your aims. No, *Verro* was about the core ideology of this stupid war. To think that precisely *how* a population told stories about itself could galvanise it to point thermo nuclear weapons at another population that told its self-narrative a differing way. Verro, well it cleared all that up didn't it? it wasn't bloodless. it never is.

[Redacted 4 seconds]

So, you are not American? ███████ perhaps? ███████ maybe? You sound American?

[detainee laughter, low audibility]

Verro spread spores, you spread language. Both warp ideas *da?* You talk like an American, you think like an American, yet you say you are not American. Fascinating.

Hmm? well Yes, at first the aim was simple; how best could we isolate the spores of the *Helminthosporium turcicum* fungus and increase their resilience. Perhaps, as the first step on the path to a potential weapon against the thriving corn belt of the Midwest, I admit. It is no secret that ██████ was keen on the development of biological arms. But mostly we conducted experimentation as a way of testing the tolerable limits of a strain that had decimated our food stock. You see, up until this crucial stage in the research, the fungus had sustained a remarkable ability to shrug off nearly all interventive, even those aggressive enough to kill the host corn.

It might be worth noting that the exact progenitor of the troublesome *Turcicum* strain was unknown. Under magnification, it closely resembled the native strain of blight with slight variations in spore size. There were some amongst the less experienced biologists in the high committee that…

Well. ████ and ████████ I'm sure you are aware of, news of their defection travelled fast, but Pulyov* and Mark-André* are both, again as you are aware, dead, long before the recent developments. And really, the names of the soviet science committee are rather irrelevant now. Wouldn't you think?

*Transcription Note: detainee speaks in reference to *Jacob Pulyov* #25 -403 Target confirmed Deceased 12/2/85 & Mark-André Martineau #28 -403 Target confirmed Deceased See record PI-28/25-403/K 18 D*

Quite…

Few of us believed the internal rumours that the blight itself was some sort of American bioweapon we were, in fact, reverse engineering. But the more experienced members that understood the nature of our soil, the truth of the earth of our nation, hypothesised simply that this blight had existed in the caucuses for hundreds of years.

[Subject takes a sip of water, silence 17 seconds]

Though, of course, few dared declare it openly, most knew it was the rush to mechanised agriculture without a proper understanding of soil ecology that had brought this beast to the surface as it were.

[interrogator question [redacted] 32 seconds]

Yes, the major obstacle with the research was isolating the particular spores in the vast interconnected ecosystem of the fungal biome that made the average Georgian cornfield thrive or die. It was in this phase of experimentation that we found the particular strain that would be the zenith of our biological armament framework. It was. I was one of the first to identify the strain as yet unknown,

[interrogator question: inaudible]

sorry? Yes, in the Russian it is Istina Zemli, quite elegant no?

*transcription note Cyrillic notation (истина земли) *

Verro terrare in its Latin. Apologies, I shall try and stick to English, but the reasons. The story behind the naming is quite...

[Interrogator question [redacted] 7 seconds]

As I have said... As I have iterated before in our previous conversations. I cannot, nor wish to, take any credit for the later developments of the spores. The... weapon itself was developed in laboratory 37. Out near Yakutsk. Even the name I can only take partial credit for.

*Transcription Note: First Direct reference to of Theta Desig. Target *Laboratory 37 Yakutsk* See record PT-65-680/K 22 D*

The queer effects of my first accidental exposure to it generated a sudden and short-lived compulsion to articulate the word 'Pravda'... sorry... 'Truth' in the English. So, at first, I wished to call it simply 'Pravda' anglicised of course,

*Transcription note: 'Pravda' Cyrillic notation 'правда' *

but that would prevent any Latin name from becoming analogous to the Cyrillic. So

[interrogator question [redacted] 11 seconds]

Well, a colleague of mine. Tasked with monitoring the effects of my brief exposure, for what more was he to do than observe and note? Ha-ha

[Subject takes a sip of water, silence 4 seconds]

Hmm Yes, He suggested that... er what was it? 'No mere mushroom could give, or be said to give, absolute truth. For what would be left for men to discover through endeavour! But a mushroom surely knew the truth of the earth of which it was a part, and maybe that was enough?'

Quite a profound man, one of the greatest minds of the...

[Interrogator Question: [redacted] 4 seconds]

His name? Incidental to... Well, I understand he is no longer with us. Your colleague █████ explained...

[Interrogator Question: [redacted] 2 seconds]

Artoym... His name was Artoym, and he was a good man, a brilliant man.

*Transcription Note: detainee speaks in reference to: *Sokolov, Artoym* #72 -404 Deceased 16/8/87 See record PI-72-404/K 18 D*

Brilliant. a true loss. well, once the effects of the spores had worn off, that particular notion stayed with me. My colleague. Artoym, graciously accepting I had contributed the most to its discovery via my exposure, allowed me to name it 'Istina Zemli' which was deliciously analogous to both the Latin 'Verro Terrare' and the English phrase 'Truth of the earth.' I am unsure to this day whether such a discovery would have garnered me international acclaim. Even if the Nobel prize committee still existed. And this is of course somewhat wistful thinking given my current... But then you see we had a rather different perspective on the discovery of Verro. There was much champagne at the announcement then. Do you understand the rarity of real champagne in the Soviet Bloc? Of course, the Nobel committee had never introduced a general category for Biology, and I assume the later development of our discovery into a bioweapon would preclude any nominations in the category of peace or physiology. Though I suppose *Verro* did lead to peace, of a fashion. Well, from a purely objective perspective, of course.

[silence 19 seconds]

Well. Nevertheless, upon hearing about the strange properties of *Verro terrare,* it is said that Khrushchev…

[Interrogator Question: [redacted] 8 seconds]

Yes, well, in a way. We were in communication, of a fashion. Not directly. Not at that point. I only ever met comrade… Mr Khrushchev… once. That was much later. Though there would be. Must be official communications to support my… um disclosure. So yes, Khrushchev, he issued the 'request' to study and isolate the strain with great fervour. I at first was reticent to abandon my research on the blight, aware of the great gains in yield efficiency that an eradication of the blight fungus would achieve. It was a time when one did not disobey the edict of the politburo and expect to keep one's place in the… to say… the scheme of things.

It is probably worth mentioning that the particular qualities of *Verro* were at first considered fairly mediocre. The spores themselves exuded a coating similar chemically to the psychoactive psilocybin. It is… if you were unaware, I'm not sure. Psilocybes have been used for their hallucinatory properties for centuries. The agaric form first categorised in the late eighteen hundred. While we understood the active agent psilocin to be produced in fruiting bodies of over two dozen species of mushroom native to the state. We had never before seen such concentration of the active compound in the mycelial matter and spore cases in this case the active hallucinogen was fused to a secondary methyl compound that slowed its hepatic metabolism allowing…

[Interrogator Question: [redacted] 4 seconds]

Put simply then. It allowed the chemical to exist in its active state beyond the blood-brain barrier for far longer than its more aggressive chemical cousin. Traditional Psilocybin could be metabolised by the liver in even the highest doses in a matter of days.

Yes, from what I recall, what made *Verro* peculiar however was that the flesh of these tiny white mushrooms upon analysis contained little of this augmented hallucinogen. All of the active chemicals were bound up in the minute fronds of the microscopic spores. So, our first step was to find ways of inducing stress to the complete organism in an attempt to increase the density of these casing fronds. After the first 18 months of trials, we had succeeded in developing a strain of the fungus that created spores that appeared under magnification like tiny horse chestnuts.

Experiments in lesser primates exhibited extreme demulcent properties. The macaques became profoundly disinterested in nearly all stimuli to the point of a waking stupor. I took no part in the rounds of human testing. Those tests, like weapon development, took place far in the north in laboratory 37. And it wasn't until 1956 that my team and I were called to central committee to hear about the plan that would turn the tide of the war.

[silence for 1 minute 24 seconds]

It was not as if I could have dissented to the plan. *Verro* was property of the state. Yes, of course, I cannot deny that its initial discovery and name are the work of my team and me. My input in that I cannot deny. But if I could stress once more, the weaponization of the strain was undertaken at lab 37, the research centre in Yakutsk, near the detention centre. I could not be compelled to go to Yakutsk, two kinds of men ended up in the permafrost of 37. Those too difficult to reform but too valuable to dispose of and those for whom the boundaries we hold sacred as scientists and humanists are trivialities, obstacles even. Neither My team nor I had any idea of what would happen to *Verro* at 37. I want that to be known. I cannot speak to it.

[Interrogator question [redacted] 1 minute 12 seconds, minimal detainee response]

Your Dr [redacted] or even [redacted] would be better placed to speak to that question. You and your helicopters swooped in to detain me before I could undertake any meaningful study on the samples at hand. It was not as if there was a newsworthy explosion or rocket launch, Verro is… was… never designed to be that kind of weapon. I'm sure they tried, but that is simply not what the biology of the fungus will allow.

I think. If I am to be candid. Not that I have much choice in the current circumstances. That the error in the soviet plan was the assumption that the ideology Verro sought to challenge was in any way different to the ideology existing on the eastern side of the wall in terms of its faith requirement. Or perhaps that a living organism designed with such a purpose would respect the arbitrary lines we call borders. We know the weapon would succeed in undermining the sense of individualism that drove the success of capitalism, what is capitalism after all but the un-shakeable belief in the invisible, intangible forces of the 'market'. profit before everything, commerce before everyone. No? But the arrogance that socialism as an ideal could be somehow im-mune to an agent that dissolved belief so completely…

Interrogator question [redacted] 48 seconds

less of a matter of my opinion Mr [redacted] I can conclude by the number of months I have been a guest of this facility with its circulated air, heavily armed personnel, and hermetically sealed rooms that the situation outside of wherever we are is tantamount to chaos. This is regrettable, all suffering is regrettable, though inevitable. Who among us is truly capable of coping once the tether to the structures we define as 'reality' are unmoored unexpectedly?

Interrogator Question [redacted] 3 seconds

No, no work was done at Lab 19 on the eradication of the blight once we were re-tasked on encouraging its properties. And after whatever processes were undertaken at that forsaken place in Yakutsk, I severely doubt that any fungicide would be capable of….

Interrogator Question [redacted] 2 seconds

In short, no. I do not think it would be reversible. Especially, as you well know, once the spores are inherent in the body the fungus continues to propagate amongst the inoculated tissue. In the variant eventually unleashed people are as effective carriers as the soil despite the lack of fruiting bodies.

Interrogator Question [redacted] 14 seconds

How? the mechanism I am sure has been well studied by now and besides this is ground we have walked before Mr. █████ repetition for the sake of...

Interrogator Question [redacted] 2 seconds

Well then. For posterity and because I do not wish it to be said I was an uncooperative guest...*Verro*, you could say... um... impedes that part of the brain we have cultivated over millennia of civilisation. The part of us that puts premiere the sense of belief that drives much of action.

Subject takes a sip of water, clears throat 11 seconds

Hm... Yes. It would be accurate to say there is extensively limited capacity for belief in the mind of the affected. With some rare cognitive impairments like lapses of object permanence. it is similar to the way a chimpanzee capable as it may of solving complex puzzles and using tools, even learning human sign language will still rarely if ever choose the option of two promised apples tomorrow when placed against the option of one apple already in its grasp. Do you see? It is a remarkably simple shift. all that seems relevant to the inoculated mind is that which is readily verifiable. Its effects are less profound in those like me already exposed to the weaker strain. But in the weaponised version the loss of 'faith' must be profound. Especially amongst those bourgeoisie masses who placed their sense of meaning entirely in ideas with little to nothing objectively concrete.

Imagine if you will the sensation of a man. An achiever of the 'American dream' who wakes up one day to realise that the job he is getting dressed for makes no sense. He has never truly understood or taken the time to understand what it is he does, and now he is incapable of reconciling the unpleasant actions he does for twelve hours a day, six days a week at the office with anything tangible. Now he comes to think of it he does not really comprehend why he does get up so early, leaving the warmth of his bed to go to this office to do this job he neither understands nor likes. There must have been a reason before, because he has many memories of doing just such a thing. But none of those reasons seem relevant now and he would much rather watch television. Then when the man on the television says that the red soviet from Russia will destroy his way of life and he should be afraid, he cannot escape the sensation that he has no idea where Russia is, has no real concept of whatever entity a soviet is and does not know the man on the TV as any different from the stranger on the street. Why should he be afraid of these things any more than he is afraid of the monsters he remembers believing were under his bed as a child? He turns it off to read the paper, something else he remembers he enjoys, though now he does not recognise many of the terms in the paper he reads either. He does not know the man referred to as 'mayor', so why should he care what this other man thinks or feels? whether he lies or does not lie? He of course remembers his wife and his children, why would he not? Verro has no effect on the centres for memory, simply altering our present interpretation of those memories. When his wife and children receive him with love and affection, he returns it. Why would he not? He has no reason to question such positive reinforcement, no reason to question the rush of endorphins and oxytocin released at his wife's embrace. It feels good ergo they are good.

The problem comes only when the man no longer turns up to work for the job that no longer seems real. And neither does the woman who authorises his pay cheque or the person at the bank who fills in the paperwork required to move the funds. When the connection between the illustrated pieces of paper in his wallet and the food he is hungry for at the store fades. When his reasoning for not simply taking the food and other things he wants fades, and the rationale that the uniformed officers have for stopping him taking the things he wants dissolve with them. The problem comes only, when the only things keeping a man from becoming a monster is the strength of his belief in the ideas that make up his society. 'I should not kill because god would judge me'. 'I should not rape because rape is a taboo that my peers would ostracise me for' et cetera.

Interrogator question 17 seconds

No. I am not saying that Verro was designed to induce homicidal tendencies. It is a fungus Mr. ███████ what behaviours it is capable of inducing in the host are behaviours the host is already capable of. What I am saying is that most of us will never meet God. Not a God in the sense any of us still capable of such beliefs believe in. Most of us on the correct side of the thin line between human and inhuman acts avoid transgressing that boundary, not because we believe it would be wrong to do so but because we understand that to be a victim of such acts would be terrible. We can empathise with the pain and terror that would cause and would not wish to inflict that experience on others. But there are enough of us, kept in check purely by that belief. Belief that we will face judgement, whether institutional or divine. People for which the notion that those acts will cause others harm comes a distant second to the thought that they will provide them selfish immediate pleasure. Verro drew a hard line between, for instance, those who fed the hungry because they understood the pain of an empty stomach and those that fed the hungry because they believed it would gain them moral capital. It is those people, that second group, unmoored from the ideas that kept them moral beings… I would conjecture that Verro turned such people into living bombs.

Even from the position of relative isolation you collected me from I could see the burning towns on the horizon. I assume Moscow went dark. Economies in every effective nation ground to a halt. What value has credit or debit or even the tokens of currency outside of a belief in their value? Which army would mobilise to lethal force against another for any other reason than a belief in the imminent threat to their nation. If humankind at large is so enamoured with killing why must nations spend so much time and resource on training their soldiers to do it, and more time and resources dealing with the fragments of their psyche after the fact?

That being said, the loss, the fear that accompanied such an awakening would have been terrible to experience outside of the comforts of a laboratory. A waking nightmare of uncertainty and confusion. Such a violently forced pragmatism. The sudden realisation that every article of faith ceases to be recognisable. Ideas from the notion of God to the Nation State becoming ridiculous, ungraspable, over a matter of hours of exposure. I'm sure that sudden loss brought out the very worst in many people. For that, the suffering that must have caused I am terribly sorry for my part in.

But the fruit? What must eventually rise from the ashes of such a conflagration, when the fires both literally and metaphorically die down? well, that, I think. May be quite beautiful. Don't you think?

End of Tape

The End of *Everything*

Omens

I

I am enjoying a quiet moment in the kitchen of a single floor villa by the sea. It is not mine, but I am living there. There is good coffee & the sound of the waves. My wife has gone to the morning market in the village to buy fresh fruit and eggs. I take in the silence of the room. I enjoy my coffee, terracotta warm beneath bare feet. I know it is a dream because the open book in front of me is an exceptionally good book I have not yet finished; it tells me it is an exceptionally good book despite its lack of words. I sip my coffee & watch a green jewel of a beetle flick its wing cases & bask in a sunbeam. It is joined by a second beetle, then a third. They form a pattern in their dance that is familiar to me, but I cannot place why. Then they leave, skittering off through the open door just as I notice a low rumble. The rumble is followed by a crack & the opposite end of the villa from the one I am sitting in begins to collapse. Before I can cry out half of the house has tumbled into the sea & I stand with my coffee in the ruin of a kitchen. I think of how I will explain this to my wife.

II

I am in a meeting somewhere stale & corporate. I am wearing a suit the colour & texture of vacuum dust. In tubular steel chairs around a square room sit members of my family. I am in a corner, my Mother to my left & my Brother to my right. My mother's side whom I love are arrayed around my half of the room & along the opposite walls, my father's side from whom I am estranged. My Father, a petty tyrant of a man is rustling paper. His youngest brother, my Uncle a man whom I had so much love for in life, is speaking. He is saying something important, vital even. As I make to write it down in the pad that is now in my lap, with the pen that is now in my hand the ink skitters leiden frost off the page. I can barely hear my Uncle over the noise of my Father rustling paper. I shout into the noise for him to stop rustling, saying something like "are you done?" & it reverberates in the room that I see has no ceiling. Only grey walls reaching up into darkness. He does not stop, so I plead, the rustling & crackling of paper deafening now. A wall of white noise & he replies something belittling & cruel but without words. A retort that cuts deeply & I snap. Rising from my seat & lunging towards him across the room. But with each stride the room becomes larger, the distance further & the rustling is now a roar of static & no one will look at me & now I know it's a dream because there is no door on either of the four walls, the room is endless & I am running, thrashing & screaming into the roar.

But, After Peckham...

White tail roam / the marsh grass edge /
bolting at the sniff / of dog pack from the scent /
marked equilateral of a give way / sign visible
above the firming mire / when Walthamstow / returned
to estuary / Epping forest / trickled its quiet life
over investment firms / in the triplet isle
of the city / growth trickled over Woodford
low rise / concrete working its way back to screed
like the white trickled out /of Brixton / once gated
entrances / were inaccessible without
earth movers & the quiet
the very texture / of the quiet / in all the years
I never thought I'd hear.

If cows were a country

I would rather be a grass fed
cow than a wild wolf.

Is it so wrong to yearn
for a short and happy life?

Over struggle, shrugged
against the cold & hunger

of a wild open? Cows have
brotherhood too. A pack

that hunt together is no less
strongly bound than one

that ruminates & grazes.
Let the being bind them rather

than the killing. Then, at the end
of things a bolt from the blue.

No matted fur, starvation or
ostracization. Simply beef.

But, After Smethwick...

There are / wild horses in Sandwell Valley
some say / they come down from the Barr
& then each winter they return
the grazing good / the streets are
sadder / they clear homes as they
fall to keep / the City rats/ big as
dogs / from finding litter / nothing
really ended here / the wall that keeps
the wound of M5 / from seeping / holds
fast / gardens spread / like bad ideas / we
work so that the land / can go to use /
 Mr. Farhadi knows / tomato & squash /
 like you know your mother's smile /
boy / you best listen.

Oblivion Hymn #4

No birth, nor coming death.
Just cosmic states that build
& pass like weather through
deep time. Imagine, three billion years
of summer rain. I'm trying to say
after all this, that something
else will come. Then after that perhaps
comes something more. The point
(if any must be made)
is nothing really ends
but nothing stays the same.

Everybody's Gone to the Rapture.

Last Thursday, 'round four in the afternoon everyone heard a voice. When I say everyone, I'm serious. I heard it. You must have? Clocked off early, was owed time, so I was in the car when it spoke. An even, sad, sigh in the head of every person and probably dog. This voice, filled with remorse, quiet as close conversation but at the same time painfully loud.

'I'm sorry. I messed up. I'll be going now.'

That was it. Nothing special. Then the lights changed, so I just followed the traffic.

To be honest, I can't say for sure whether the voice spoke in every language. It's only Tuesday and no one knows which of the mass of reports are legit. Some Russians online said they were woken up in the middle of the night, which would make sense, time zones and that. But you've got to be wary of the Russians, haven't you? Besides, like I said, it's only Tuesday, and a lot of people still don't have much of an opinion on the voice.

I know that in the traffic, in that muddled bit at the end of the school run but before the rush hour, the voice didn't stop cars. Woman in the car next to me was arguing on hands free. The kids in the back were looking around trying to figure out where it was coming from, but their mum, I assume she was their mum, didn't even seem to notice.

So even if everybody heard it at the same time, not everybody gave a shit, but we're pretty sure now that the voice also spoke to dogs.

'The apology' was Thursday afternoon and by Friday, every dog in the neighbourhood just stopped giving a damn. I heard from the neighbours how they just helped themselves to treats when they felt like them, ignored commands, pissed wherever they felt like it. So, when your dog is bad, what do you do? Round here you stick them outside in the back garden.

Wasn't long before most people realised that was exactly what Fido or Spot was after. Soon as they were outside, every dog that could either jumped their fences or dug under them. Sometimes it was hours before people even noticed they were gone.

Reddit started calling it 'The apology' which I guess it was, and it was all over the news. But like I said, it was met first by a collective nothingness. I don't think I mentioned it to Laura until after dinner, and even then, it was with something like: 'What was all that about? Weird wasn't it?' And she didn't really have much to say, just carried on washing up while I dried the casserole dish. She stayed quiet, I worried I'd fucked up somehow, come home with beer on my breath or something. But I knew I was alright, I was even helping clean up, so I knew it wasn't that. Figured later that it was the end of the world. It makes people weird.

Anyway, no one really said or did anything about it until the Friday night when the first tweets began to circulate. Some ironically attached to the tag #SoLongAndThanksForAllTheFish. from some sci-fi apparently, 'Hitchhikers' or something -too many memes to keep up with- I popped up on Netflix suggested but I never got round to watching it. Buzzfeed did a 'poll' of emoji reactions to the voice. The second most selected emoji was the eggplant.

So, up until the weekend it was all a bit of a laugh if anything. Laura was less quiet than she had been Thursday night. Snuck out for a smoke in the garden Saturday morning when I thought she'd gone to bed. Scared the shit out of me. She sat there at 3am on the phone to her mum, crying and I'm thinking 'shit! What's happened? Has someone died? Has her dad died?' We didn't always see eye to eye me and her dad, but he was alright. Top bloke after a few whiskeys, and he wasn't a twat about drinking around me like others were.

But she just said, 'It's fine Steven, go back to bed.' I hadn't been to bed. *Field of Fire* had a double XP event, and I was gagging for a smoke. But she called me by my full name, So I knew I was on thin ice. She always hated me smoking. I cut down, but she hated it.

'The apology' broke twitter. Mostly through people *memeing* the shit out of it all. But by Sunday the lol's and murmurings were buried under the weight of the suicide footage. I should say, *attempted* suicides.

Some evangelical church in Guatemala was supposedly the first to recognise it as the voice of God. I say recognise, it's not as if we'd heard the voice before. I mean we sort of had.. The voice was familiar. Not in a warm home way, not quite a gut punch either. Like hearing a laugh in the bustle of a pub. And you swear that's the laugh of an ex, someone who really left their claws in you, but you've finally blanked her face, and you know only she laughed like that, only it can't be her, 'cause it's been 10 years now. And you saw before she blocked you on Facebook that she's living in Barcelona now with some property developer with shiny teeth. And, besides, you can't see her anywhere, and why the fuck would she be in a pub in Bromford? You know what I mean?

Anyway, all these worshippers, they all heard the voice and decided that they really didn't want to live in a world without their almighty. I get it. If you've been praying to this silence all these years, and you really believed in all that, it might come like a bad joke when the one time your God speaks it's to say that He's tapping out and not coming back. Would take the piss wouldn't it? But I reckon they took it a bit far.

Whipped into it by their Padre they figured the best thing to do would be to make a dignified and ceremonial mass exit from life. so, of course, because it's the 21st century they livestreamed the whole affair. I guess it's one way to prove your devotion, isn't it? But to who I'm not sure. 'cause God had wandered off, hadn't they? So, he wasn't around to impress.

I haven't been in a church since my christening, got married in a registry office then went to the pub. But even I know suicide will fuck your chances of getting into heaven, so I'm not sure what they were playing at.

It's like trying to top yourself when your girlfriend walks out. You only screw yourself. If you pull it off, you're dead and she isn't coming back.

In any case, only a handful of people bothered to actually watch the live suicide. I didn't, but those that did probably logged in out of macabre self-interest. The full stream was over an hour long, only the last 7 minutes or so were actually suicide. So, I didn't bother to watching live. It's not my thing.

By Monday millions had watched the flailing, frothing congregation. Well over 300 churchgoers, every one of them robed in brilliant white, made more brilliant by the 90s soft focus saturation filter. Every one of them shitting and fitting as they succumbed to the cyanide laced communion wine. Their choking layered underneath a tinny digital rendition of *Swing Low Sweet Chariot*. Then, after about a minute or so of perfect stillness- The music still playing cause the studio operator had killed himself too- every one of them, just... got up.

It looked ridiculous. All of them scrabbling their way up from the floor in their stained robes. Every one of them looking dazed and more than a little embarrassed, but otherwise un-hurt. Every one of them definitely alive. I'm not sure if they cut the feed straight away or let it run. I wouldn't know. Like I said it wasn't really my thing. Besides, who would spend an hour watching a botched suicide attempt? Literally, the only thing sadder than suicide?

The copy-cats have followed in waves. People really going at it, you know. People can't die, but you can still get hurt. You can *really* mess yourself up, it just, doesn't last.

I watched a guy try to take his head off with one of those hedge trimmers. It got halfway through his neck before the blood and vomit stopped the motor. The rest of the video was just him retching and wiggling the blade to get it out. But after-wards there was just a clean smear of white in the blood where a massive gash should have been.

It's almost become a bit of a meme, taking over from tide pods or something. Thought it was normal before to get some prick on a message board yelling 'GO KILL YOURSELF' in all caps? Now it's basically said as a joke. A way to shut down someone making a pointless argument. It took 2 whole days for suicide to become internet shorthand for meaninglessness. Even messed around with it myself. It was stupid. Curiosity really. Just to see what would happen. Laura didn't take kindly to it though. In fact, she absolutely lost it and I really fucked up the bathroom.

Dying isn't a thing anymore, which makes sense, in the way any of this makes sense. Nearly all the good books say some-thing along the lines of 'God giveth and God taketh away' don't they? So now there's no 'God' to taketh, I reckon it's too early to tell whether the giveth part has gone too.

It would make sense if it had, but the news feeds are too preoccupied with showy suicide performances and the thing with the dogs to tell us whether or not we can... you know. Though there has been plenty of spontaneous, often public sex. Just, Right out there, in the middle of the suburbs.

Sometimes strangers, just going at it. The end of the world will do that I suppose. Make people weird.

So, for now babies are a maybe, I guess we will find out in a couple of months, wont we? It is what it is.

Maybe the dogs had the right idea of it? See, I reckon they heard the voice too because of the way they started acting. The sudden exodus.

Laura and I don't have a dog, we were going to adopt one once we got a house with a garden, but never got round to it. Well… we got the house.

Matt and Jeremy next door, lovely guys, they have a pug and a cat. The cat is still there, fat, and nonchalant as ever, but the pug slipped the leash on her morning walk on Friday. Matt was picking up after her, he says, and wasn't holding tight. The clever bitch must have been waiting for the moment and just took off, trailing her little tartan lead behind her as she bolted.

It's not Matt's fault. I reckon that little pug knew the hurt she would cause, and she left anyway. It's been 4 days now. And you know what, I'm happy for her. I really am. I hope she's happy.

I'm glad we never got a dog. I think it's still a bit much for Matt. I could see him weeping from the bathroom window. I wasn't lurking, it was raining. I wasn't going to smoke outside, was I? I'm half out the window and he's just standing. There, in his garden, in the pouring rain. He's lit by those little LED stick lights they had the landscaper put in, just bawling, sobbing loud enough to hear through the open window. I could see him, standing with this little green rubber bone in his hand, every now and then he'd form a fist around it and just, squeak it, softly, and carry-on crying.

Jeremy tried to bring him in, but they ended up just standing there together, in the rain. All I'm thinking is, it's been four days man. It was just a dog. End of the world, it's made people weird.

Mellissa, I think her name was. shit name for a Pug.

On the 6 o' clock news there are reports of all sorts, Labradors and Chihuahuas muddling along together in the New forest. Some PDSA bloke got chunks ripped out of him trying to bring in a group of ex police Alsatians. What did he expect would happen? Even the daytime news is accompanied by 'miraculous new dog stories', grainy night footage of them hunting rabbits or padding through open fields or whatever. 'Miraculously' just coexisting as if not being a prick to someone a different size and shape to you is something humans invented.

I kind of feel happy for them. you know? I don't know if the dogs also can't die, but it's pretty smart of them to realise that there's little point being a "good boy" or "good girl" if there is no heaven to be "good" for. And anyway, being "good" was really just following random rules that we came up with for our entertainment. Poor sods must have been playing along for years. Putting up with our nonsense, accepting our petty authority until "the apology", and then they didn't have to anymore. Fair play to them really.

To be honest I'm more worried about the state of things once humans figure out what the dogs have already cottoned on to. There're some really murky opinions online if you're willing to look. But it'll probably be fine.

Can't get any worse than the end of the world, can it? Things with Laura will sort themselves out, I'm sure.

She was all 'what is wrong with you?' And 'you fucking promised' 'why would you even try do this to us again?'. It didn't matter that it's not the same now. It didn't leave a mark this time, and I knew it wouldn't, we both did, so it's not even slightly the same. It did make a mess. But that was only 'cause I panicked and splashed around. I didn't realise that you had to pretty much bleed out, it's not something you think through sober. And for a mad minute, I just thought 'shit, what if I'm the only one who *can* die.' And I panicked. Which was stupid to be honest. I'm not that special.

So, it wasn't all that bad was it. The world might have ended, whatever that means? But when you think about it, at least now we know that God *was* real, and however messy it got, nobody died.

Laura's at her sisters for a bit. Which is fair, I guess. I should've known better.

Ordered some new grout and a couple of scrapers. I really did fuck up the bathroom.

Acknowledgements

The Author would like to thank his family in Blood.

Momma Avis for allowing the Library to be a second home for all those years. His brother Alex for being the Protagonist, Antagonist & Co-conspirator in a thousand stories that will never be written down. Nanna Ricketts, the source of all stories, the oracle, the chronicle & the only person I've ever met on casual terms with the Almighty.

Also, his family in Ink.

Sisters Naush Sabah & Suna Afshan for casting their eyes over countless lines, applying their skills to tightening paragraphs & voicing the lesser heard. Brother Casey Bailey for holding the flame for lyricism & craft in our shared corner of the world (0121). The School of English at Birmingham City university, Particularly the diligent support of Professor Gregory Leadbetter & Dr Sarah Wood. Two lecturers amongst a fantastic group of teachers who encouraged me to break things, take risks & read beyond. Publisher Aaron Kent for seeing enough in my previous scribbles to support the crafting of the strange hybrid thing you have just read.

& last, but furthest from the least Vinita, fourth born of tall bamboo & a governors daughter. My heart & the first reader for every sentence. There are no words without you love.

LAY OUT YOUR UNREST